To the players who integrated pro football,
and the artists who recognize the beauty of sports.
—S. N. W.

To anyone who takes the time to make a big deal
out of seeing beauty in small moments.
—B. C.

All quotes contained in this book are actual Ernie Barnes quotes and are taken from Ernie Barnes's book *From Pads to Palette* or from interviews detailed in the back matter.

The author gratefully acknowledges the Ernie Barnes Family Trust for allowing reproductions of the following paintings to be used in this book:

The Bench by Ernie Barnes, 1959. Acrylic on canvas 20 x 37 inches.
Collection of the Pro Football Hall of Fame. All rights reserved. Used by permission.

Double Dutch by Ernie Barnes, 1990. Acrylic on canvas 23 x 29 inches.
In private collection. All rights reserved. Reprinted by permission.

My Miss America by Ernie Barnes, 1970 • Acrylic on canvas 48 x 36 inches.
Collection of the California African American Museum
All rights reserved. Reprinted by permission.

SIMON & SCHUSTER BOOKS FOR YOUNG READERS
An imprint of Simon & Schuster Children's Publishing Division
1230 Avenue of the Americas, New York, New York 10020
Text copyright © 2018 by Sandra Neil Wallace
Illustrations copyright © 2018 by Bryan Collier
All rights reserved, including the right of reproduction in whole or in part in any form.
SIMON & SCHUSTER BOOKS FOR YOUNG READERS is a trademark of Simon & Schuster, Inc.
For information about special discounts for bulk purchases, please contact Simon & Schuster Special Sales
at 1-866-506-1949 or business@simonandschuster.com.
The Simon & Schuster Speakers Bureau can bring authors to your live event. For more information
or to book an event, contact the Simon & Schuster Speakers Bureau at 1-866-248-3049
or visit our website at www.simonspeakers.com.
Book design by Laurent Linn
The text for this book was set in Chaparral Pro.
The illustrations for this book were rendered in watercolor and collage.
Manufactured in China
1117 SCP
First Edition
2 4 6 8 10 9 7 5 3 1
Library of Congress Cataloging-in-Publication Data
Names: Wallace, Sandra Neil, author.
Title: Between the lines : how Ernie Barnes went from the football field
to the art gallery / Sandra Neil Wallace ; illustrated by Bryan Collier.
Description: First edition. | New York : Simon & Schuster Books for Young Readers, 2018. |
"A Paula Wiseman Book." | Includes bibliographical references.
Identifiers: LCCN 2016010818 | ISBN 9781481443876 (hardcover : alk. paper) |
ISBN 9781481443883 (eBook)
Subjects: LCSH: Barnes, Ernie, 1938–2009. | Football players—United States—Biography. | Painters—
United States—Biography. | Football players as artists. | Civil rights movements—United States—History—
20th century. | African Americans—Civil rights—History—20th century.
Classification: LCC GV939.B376 W35 2018 | DDC 796.332092 [B]—dc23
LC record available at https://lccn.loc.gov/2016010818

BETWEEN the LINES

How
ERNIE BARNES
Went from the Football Field
to the Art Gallery

Sandra Neil Wallace

SANDRA NEIL WALLACE

Illustrated by
BRYAN COLLIER

A Paula Wiseman Book

SIMON & SCHUSTER BOOKS FOR YOUNG READERS

NEW YORK LONDON TORONTO SYDNEY NEW DELHI

ERNEST LOVED THE NORTH CAROLINA RAIN.
He waited for the backyard to turn into mud.
Painting mud. Then Ernest found a stick and
painted in the slippery soil.

He drew straight lines and curved lines.
Looped lines and crossed lines.

Lines that kept moving, past his father's
new picket fence and onto Willard Street. The
neighbors wondered what Ernest was painting.
They followed the lines to see where they led.

Mama saw how Ernest loved to paint. But in the segregated South she did not feel welcome in the art museum. So on sunny days she brought Ernest with her to work. Mama was a housekeeper for a lawyer in Durham's white section. Ernest hadn't known anyone with a library until Mr. Fuller. The room smelled of leather books and mahogany frames that Mama polished. Ernest stared at the beautiful paintings in the frames.

They told stories without words.

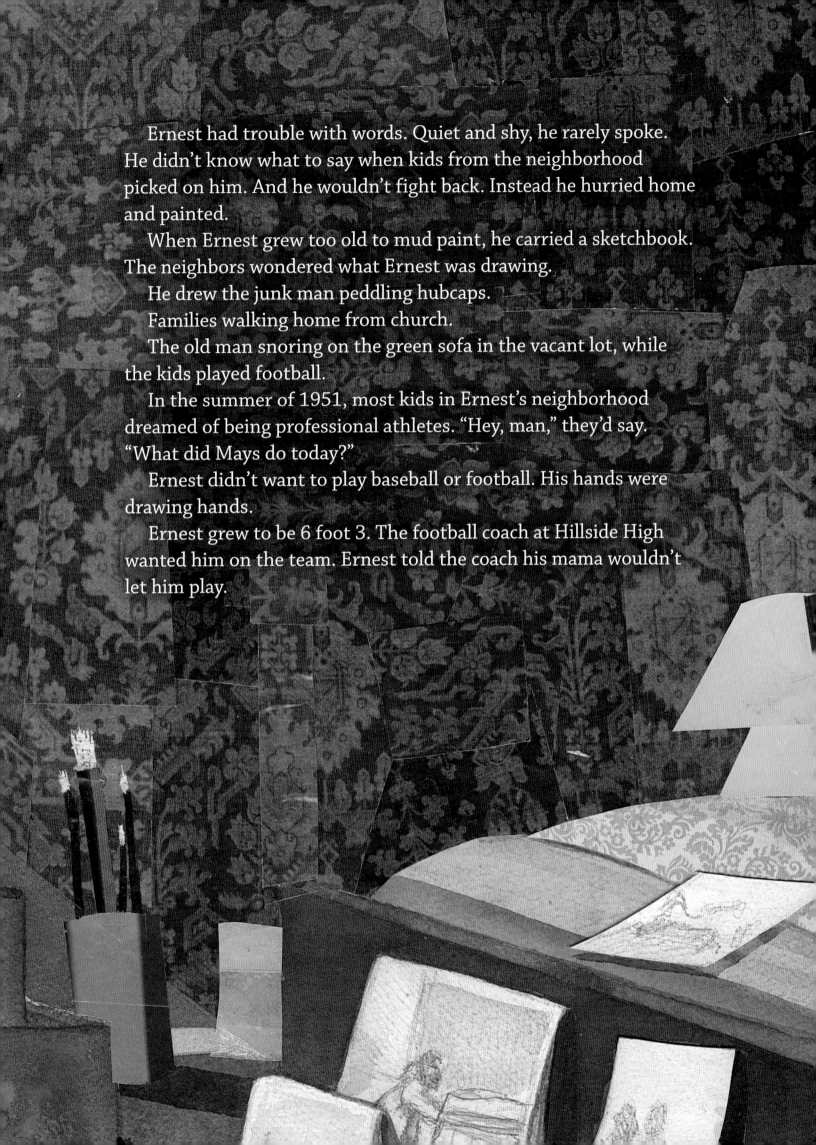

Ernest had trouble with words. Quiet and shy, he rarely spoke. He didn't know what to say when kids from the neighborhood picked on him. And he wouldn't fight back. Instead he hurried home and painted.

When Ernest grew too old to mud paint, he carried a sketchbook. The neighbors wondered what Ernest was drawing.

He drew the junk man peddling hubcaps.

Families walking home from church.

The old man snoring on the green sofa in the vacant lot, while the kids played football.

In the summer of 1951, most kids in Ernest's neighborhood dreamed of being professional athletes. "Hey, man," they'd say. "What did Mays do today?"

Ernest didn't want to play baseball or football. His hands were drawing hands.

Ernest grew to be 6 foot 3. The football coach at Hillside High wanted him on the team. Ernest told the coach his mama wouldn't let him play.

One afternoon when Ernest came home from school, he found the coach in the kitchen eating Mama's cooking. On the table was a donation for Mama's church. Ernest knew his drawing hands would soon be playing for the Hornets.

Coach made him an offensive lineman. Ernest played center, and became captain of the team.

Ernest was so good at blocking that college scouts watched him play. He was offered twenty-six scholarships. Ernest chose North Carolina College at Durham, an all-black university across the street from Hillside High. He studied art and played football.

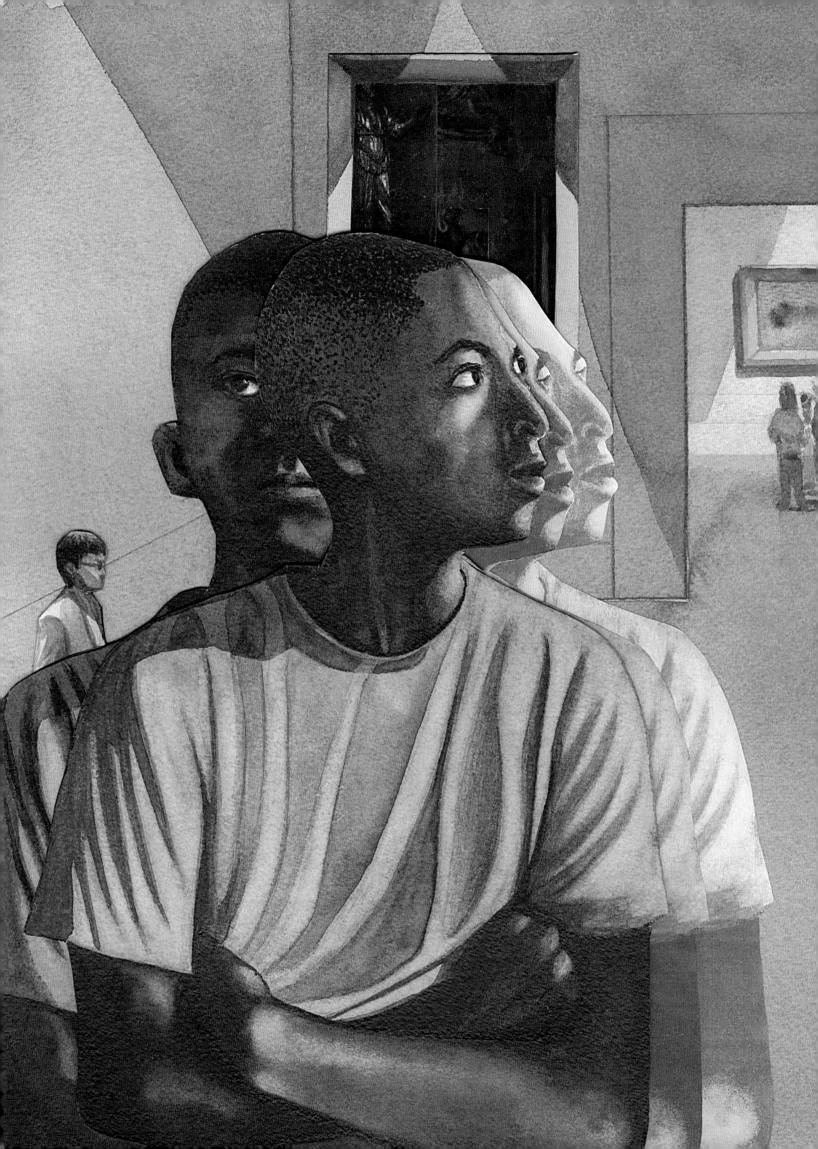

In his first year of college, the civil rights movement pushed for greater freedom for African Americans. Now Ernest and his art class could visit the museum.

Ernest searched for paintings of people like him. He didn't see any. He had to find the words to ask the tour guide an important question. Ernest moved closer, gathering the words in his head. "Where are the paintings by Negro artists?" he asked.

Surprised by Ernest's question, the tour guide paused. "Your people don't express themselves in that way," she said.

Ernest knew they did. His teacher had shown slides of artwork by Henry O. Tanner, Edmonia Lewis, and Palmer Hayden.

But what would Ernest paint? His canvas stayed blank.

His art teacher, Mr. Wilson, drove Ernest through the neighborhood. Inside the homes, Ernest knew the rhythm of laughter from his father's ragtime piano, and the hard times. Ernest and Mr. Wilson yanked up a shoe stuck in the muddy walkway. A shoe with a story to be painted, about hard times.

"Art is all around you," Mr. Wilson told Ernest. "Use what you see. You catch my drift?"

Thinking about what Mr. Wilson had said, Ernest looked around his neighborhood. It no longer appeared ordinary. In the movement of every football play . . . in the explosion of a kickoff . . . in the swivel and swerves of game action, he saw beauty.

He had found what to paint.

"Who is going to feed you if you become a painter?" asked Ernest's father.

Ernest wasn't sure.

In his senior year of college, National Football League scouts came to watch Ernest play. "We are going to draft you," they told him. But he didn't think they were serious. He had other plans.

On Draft Day in 1959, Ernest waited in Mama's kitchen. The whole day. No telegram came.

In the morning Ernest spotted his name in the newspaper. He ran outside to tell Mama. "I'm going to be in the pros!" he shouted. Ernest would earn a living playing football for the Baltimore Colts.

A few weeks later Ernest rode a bus to watch the Colts play in the NFL championship game. He heard the *thwack* of tangled linemen butting shoulders on the field. He saw the sweaty faces of his new team, who sat shoulder-to-shoulder on the bench. Players lunged forward, itching to play.

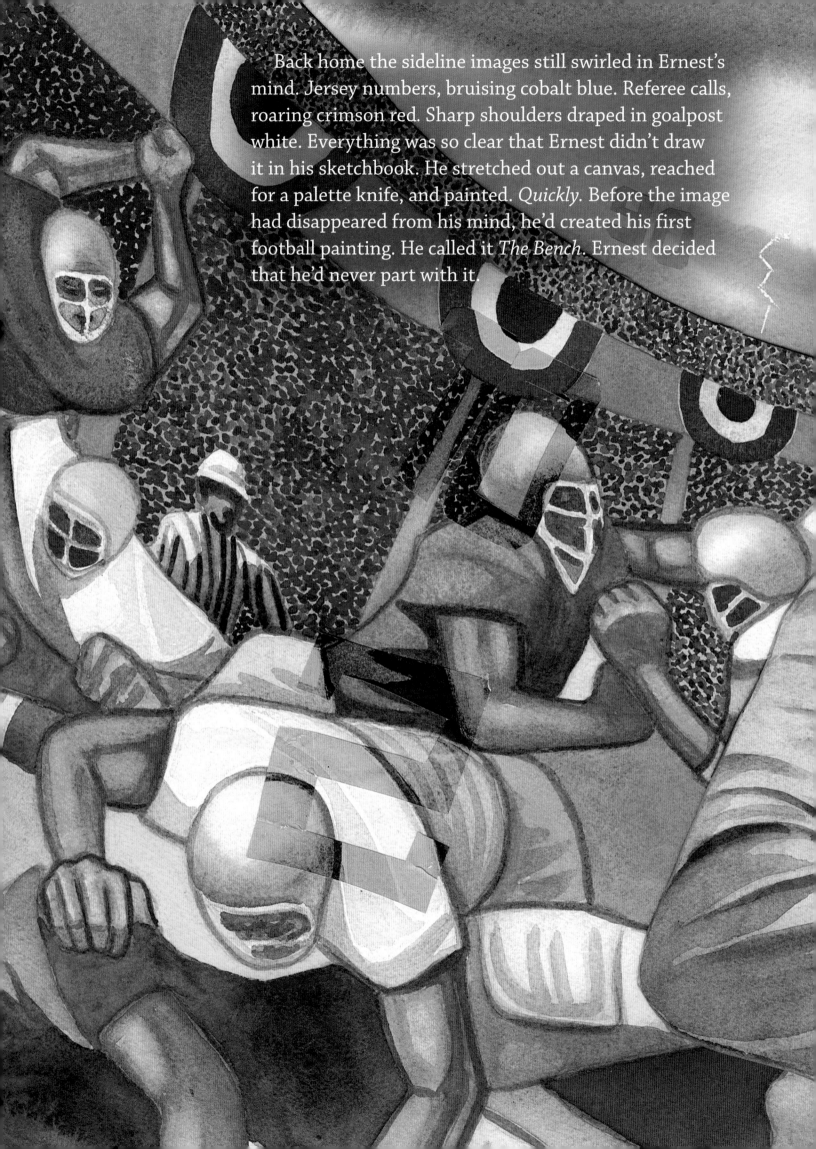

Back home the sideline images still swirled in Ernest's mind. Jersey numbers, bruising cobalt blue. Referee calls, roaring crimson red. Sharp shoulders draped in goalpost white. Everything was so clear that Ernest didn't draw it in his sketchbook. He stretched out a canvas, reached for a palette knife, and painted. *Quickly.* Before the image had disappeared from his mind, he'd created his first football painting. He called it *The Bench.* Ernest decided that he'd never part with it.

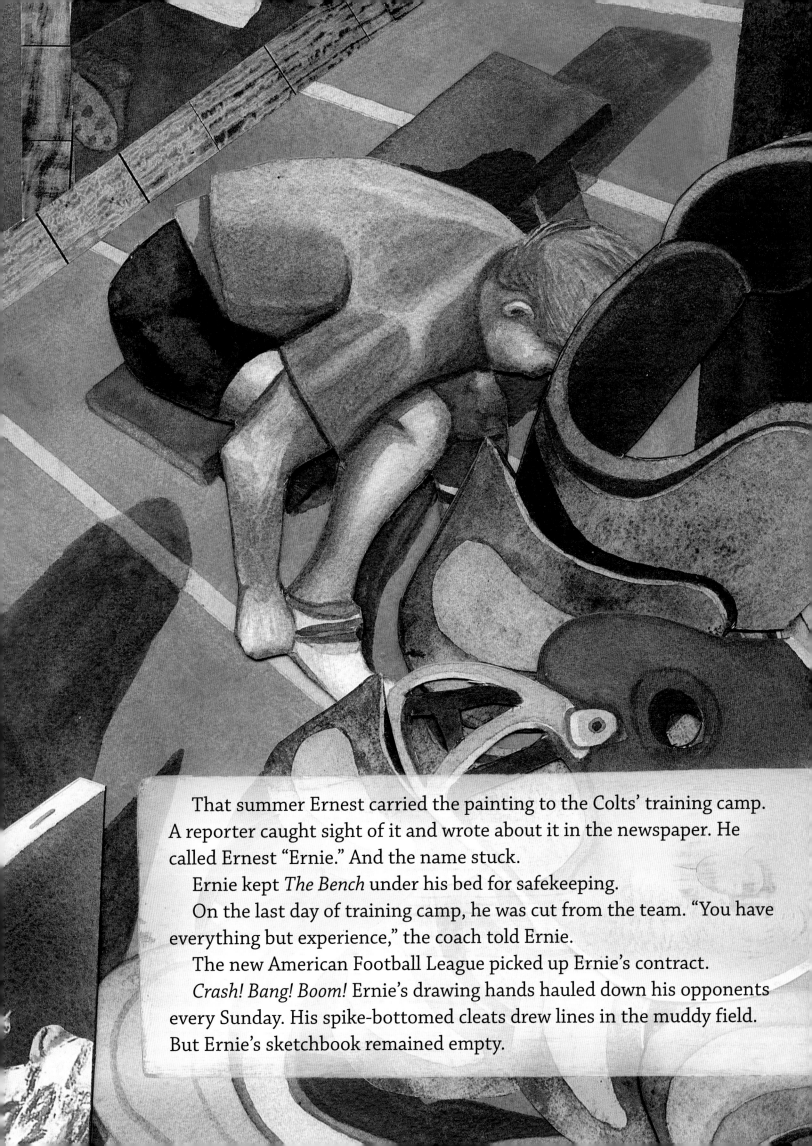

That summer Ernest carried the painting to the Colts' training camp. A reporter caught sight of it and wrote about it in the newspaper. He called Ernest "Ernie." And the name stuck.

Ernie kept *The Bench* under his bed for safekeeping.

On the last day of training camp, he was cut from the team. "You have everything but experience," the coach told Ernie.

The new American Football League picked up Ernie's contract.

Crash! Bang! Boom! Ernie's drawing hands hauled down his opponents every Sunday. His spike-bottomed cleats drew lines in the muddy field. But Ernie's sketchbook remained empty.

In a magazine, Ernie read "I Am A Negro," by Paul R. Williams. "Negroes, Wake Up!" Williams wrote. "Real Emancipation lies in your own intellectual effort." Ernie did not want to take his freedom for granted. He thought about his wish to be an artist.

Ernie longed to paint, but his fingers were too swollen from blocking. When Ernie broke his hand in a game, a cast was put on so that he could still play. Even so, the coach dropped Ernie from the team.

A want ad in the newspaper caught Ernie's attention. GOOD SALARY GUARANTEED it read. But there was no guarantee as a door-to-door salesman. Still, he took the job. He challenged himself to learn eight new words a day.

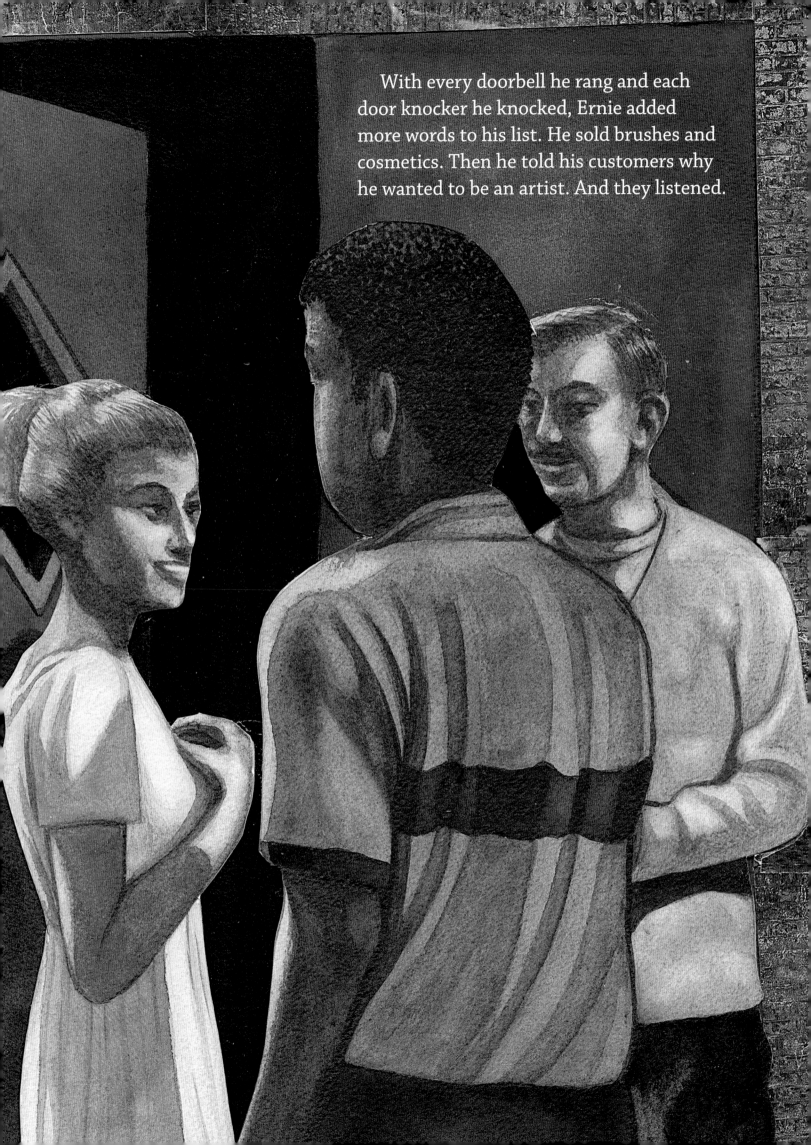

With every doorbell he rang and each door knocker he knocked, Ernie added more words to his list. He sold brushes and cosmetics. Then he told his customers why he wanted to be an artist. And they listened.

Playing football earned more money than selling brushes. So after his hand healed, Ernie joined another team. He tucked a stubby pencil and a small notepad into his football socks. During time-outs he scribbled notes about what he saw on the line of scrimmage, nicknamed "the Pit."

He saw players clawing, scrapping, reaching, fighting to win. With his swollen hands, Ernie drew lines making them stretch even farther.

Each time the coach caught Ernie sketching, he fined him fifty dollars.

Ernie kept drawing. One time when he reached for his notepad, it was gone. He watched the pieces of paper floating above the field in the wind. "Hey, Barnes!" the coach yelled. "You could be great if only you would get that art out of your head!"

In the last game of the 1964 season, it rained. The field turned into mud. *Painting mud.* Ernie studied the uniforms covered in muddy brown. Linemen surging, blocking steely blue. Clashing bodies, stinging bloody scarlet. He followed the rain up to the brooding sky, listening to the roar in the stadium. He imagined the players as gladiators in a coliseum, wearing coats of armor, fighting for their lives.

Ernie had to paint the story. After the game he told his coach he was finished playing football.

With no money for rent, Ernie painted on the stoop outside a Los Angeles motel room. He pawned watches and art books for food. He worried. Would anyone buy his paintings? Ernie needed a game plan to sell his artwork.

Leafing through a magazine, Ernie read a letter written by the famous painter Vincent van Gogh. "I have a lot of work to do, but I still have the firm hope to succeed," van Gogh had written.

Encouraged by van Gogh's words, Ernie came up with a brilliant game plan. He gathered his paintings and carried them to a meeting for the owners of the American Football League.

Ernie tapped on the microphone to get their attention. "I want to become the Official Artist for the American Football League," he began.

Someone asked Ernie a question. "When can you come to New York and bring your paintings with you?" It was Sonny Werblin, owner of the New York Jets. Sonny offered Ernie a football player's salary. But he didn't want Ernie to play. He wanted him to paint! Then Ernie would have his own show in a New York gallery.

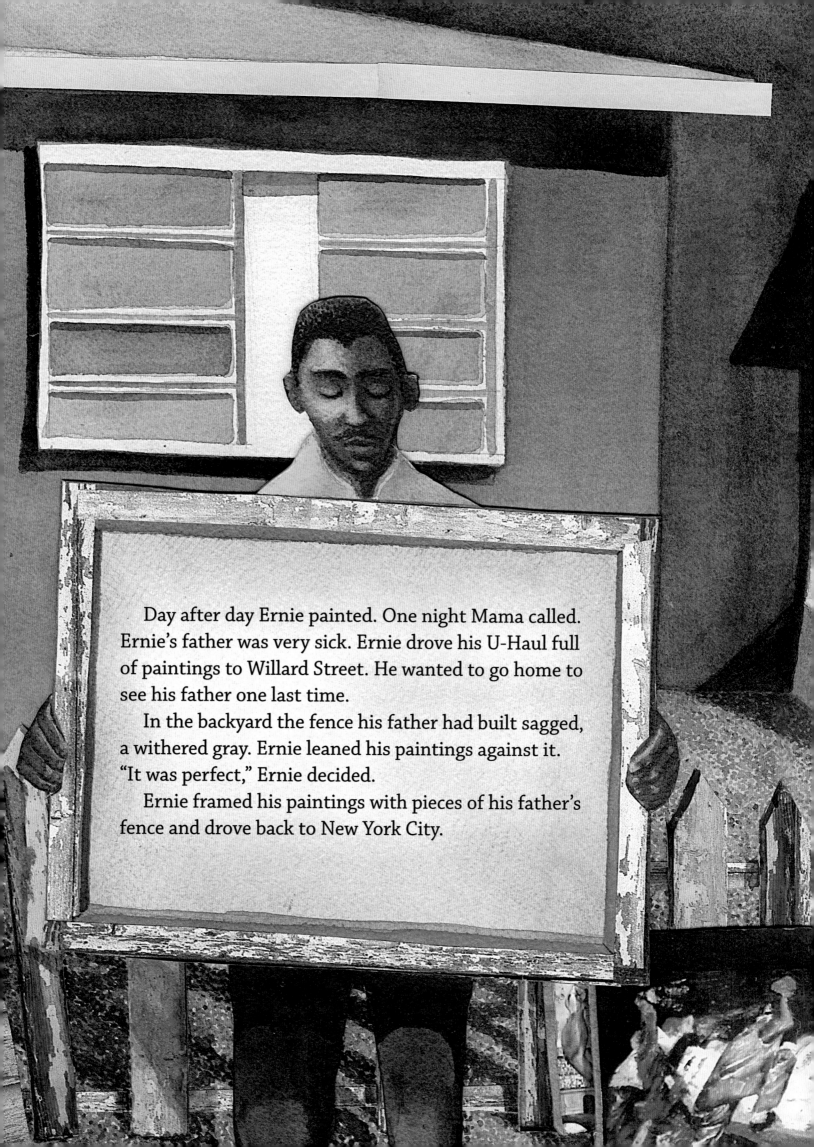

Day after day Ernie painted. One night Mama called. Ernie's father was very sick. Ernie drove his U-Haul full of paintings to Willard Street. He wanted to go home to see his father one last time.

In the backyard the fence his father had built sagged, a withered gray. Ernie leaned his paintings against it. "It was perfect," Ernie decided.

Ernie framed his paintings with pieces of his father's fence and drove back to New York City.

On the opening night of Ernie's show, the gallery buzzed with activity. Visitors marveled at what Ernie had painted. A woman stuck red SOLD stickers next to his drawings and paintings. *The Bench*—Ernie's first football painting—was not for sale. Ernie kept that as his own.

For years afterward Ernie's drawing hands painted stories. Celebrities, art lovers, and athletes pushed close to admire his paintings in galleries and museums across the country.

One day schoolchildren came to visit the museum in North Carolina. They asked to see paintings by African American artists.

The tour guide showed them the newest exhibit. The artist was Ernie Barnes.

They saw paintings of flowers growing in cracked sidewalks. They saw football players sparring like gladiators, their hopeful hands reaching for the ball. They saw dancers painted in bright dresses and blue jeans swaying to the rhythm of saxophones glinting gold. In Ernie's paintings they saw hope. They saw struggle.

They saw beauty.

When I became an athlete I didn't stop being an artist.
—ERNIE BARNES

Ernie Barnes was born on Rembrandt's birthday, July 15, in 1938. Named after his father, a tobacco clerk, Ernie grew up in the segregated South of Durham, North Carolina. That meant he didn't have equal access to museums, art galleries, or public libraries and attended all-black schools. But his mother, Fannie Mae, made certain her children knew about music and art.

She ran the household of Frank Fuller, a wealthy white lawyer, and brought home discarded classical records and art books. Ernie visited the Fullers often, where he discovered the art of sixteenth-century painters, including Michelangelo.

By the time he entered school, Ernie knew he wanted to be an artist.

Shy and sensitive, Ernie sought hiding places in school so he could sketch and avoid being bullied. A high school weight lifting coach discovered him in the halls and helped him become a star athlete.

Ernie became an offensive lineman and played pro football with three teams in the American Football League. (The American Football League merged with the National Football League in 1970.)

But ignoring his artistic dream proved frustrating. Viewing football as a contest of "beauty and grace," Ernie sketched on the sidelines, exaggerating the players' movements and shapes.

Ernie's game experience gave his work another dimension. Art critics praised him as "America's best painter of sports" since George Bellows. In 1984 Ernie became the official artist of the Olympic Games.

By then Ernie was a household name. Elevating daily life with dignified paintings of playground scenes and dance halls, his exhibit *The Beauty of the Ghetto* became the face of the Black Is Beautiful cultural movement. The exhibit toured the United States from 1972 to 1979, hosted by politicians and presidents, including Jimmy Carter.

The focal painting, *Sugar Shack*, was shown each week as part of the closing credits on the TV sitcom *Good Times*. The lead character of the show, J. J. Evans, and his aspirations of being a painter were modeled after Ernie Barnes's life. *Sugar Shack*, depicting dancers enjoying the rhythm at a jazz club, has been called one of the fifty greatest paintings in American history. When rhythm and blues artist Marvin Gaye saw the painting, he put it on his next album cover.

Ernie Barnes has been called the creator of the neo-Mannerism art movement. But to many, Barnes brought movement to art, and elevated the ordinary to the extraordinary.

Ernie Barnes died in Los Angeles on April 27, 2009, from a rare blood disorder at the age of seventy.

He never sold his first football painting, *The Bench*. It has a permanent place of honor in the Pro Football Hall of Fame in Canton, Ohio.

Today Ernie's work hangs in museums in Philadelphia; Los Angeles; New York City; Washington, DC; and Daphne, Alabama.

The Bench by Ernie Barnes, 1959 • Acrylic on canvas 20 x 37 inches. • Collection of the Pro Football Hall of Fame

═══ AUTHOR'S NOTE ═══

As an ESPN sportscaster, I had the opportunity to interview Olympic athletes. Next to their trophies and medals, there would often be posters depicting the Olympic Games. One in particular that caught my attention was from the 1984 Los Angeles Olympics titled *The Neighborhood*, by Ernie Barnes. Like the people portrayed in the painting, I had spent my childhood summers pretending to compete in the Olympics.

I didn't pay close attention to who the artist of the painting was until I read about Barnes's death in 2009. His story of excelling in professional sports yet yearning to be an artist appealed to me. So did Barnes's perseverance and commitment to developing a blueprint for success in his career of choice, despite the odds stacked against him. As a successful sports reporter, I longed to write children's books. Like Ernie's coaches, my colleagues couldn't understand why.

After I laid eyes on *The Bench*, my heartbeat quickened. I was immediately inspired by the bold brushstrokes that appear to bounce off the canvas to a rhythm, evoking a sense of purpose and attitude that carries over into all of Barnes's paintings. I became determined to tell the Ernie Barnes story.

Within a few years I'd read reviews of his work and collected a dozen art catalogs and rare photographs from his exhibits. I sourced newspaper and magazine articles dating back to 1959 on the football-player-turned-artist. I read his autobiography, amassed collectible cards, and studied his charcoal sideline sketches. Through interviews I also collected invaluable personal anecdotes from members of the Ernie Barnes Family Trust.

What I couldn't do was interview Ernie Barnes. But some believe that the soul of an artist is revealed in their work. What I see in Ernie's paintings is what he believed: that art has the capacity to change people's points of view.

—*S. N. W.*

Being an artist has created in me the desire to continually affirm beauty.
—ERNIE BARNES

ILLUSTRATOR'S NOTE

I had the pleasure of meeting Mr. Ernie Barnes at an art festival in Philadelphia about the year 2000. I found him to be an easy-to-approach gentle giant as well as a dignified statesman. As I watched the mass of onlookers who were both artists and art lovers, I realized that we were all connected and caught under the same spell—the art of Ernie Barnes. That art was introduced to so many of us in our living rooms every week through the popular 1970s television show called *Good Times*. His painting, *Sugar Shack*, was shown in the closing credits every week.

Ernie Barnes—the man, artist, and athlete—has been and still is an inspiration to many successful artists, actors, and athletes today. His journey from childhood with all his artistic gifts and promise along with growing up in the South in an era of segregation in America with all of its struggles and limitations opened the door to many. In his athletic years, Ernie found beauty in all of it, and he showed it off to the world. He proved to us that in art and football: you do not have to choose one or the other; you can choose both.

This book's art is painted in watercolor and collage and there are areas where I show you the actual art of Ernie Barnes with his signature exaggerated figures in expressive motion that lives on to inspire the world. I chose not to re-create this book in Ernie's style because it is so original and unique that it shines so proudly on its own. It speaks for itself.

—B. C.

Double Dutch by Ernie Barnes, 1990 • Acrylic on canvas 23 x 29 inches.
In private collection • All rights reserved. Reprinted by permission.

TO LEARN MORE

Barnes, Ernie. *From Pads to Palette*. Waco, TX: WRS Publishing, 1995.

Bodart, Diane. *Renaissance & Mannerism*. New York: Sterling, 2008.

Marley, Anna O., ed. *Henry Ossawa Tanner: Modern Spirit*. Oakland: University of California Press, 2012.

Smith, Thomas G. *Showdown: JFK and the Integration of the Washington Redskins*. Boston: Beacon Press, 2012.

FOR YOUNG READERS

Burleigh, Robert. *George Bellows: Painter with a Punch!* New York: National Gallery of Art/ Abrams, 2012.

Hudson, Karen E. *The Will and the Way: Paul R. Williams, Architect*. New York: Rizzoli, 1994.

Winter, Jonah, and Terry Widener. *You Never Heard of Willie Mays?!* New York: Schwartz & Wade, 2013.

Wolfe, Rinna Evelyn. *Edmonia Lewis: Wildfire in Marble*. Parsippany, NJ: Silver Burdett Press, 1998.

WEBSITE

Official website of artist Ernie Barnes: www.erniebarnes.com

VIDEOS

"Black Is Beautiful." *The African Americans: Many Rivers to Cross* with Henry Louis Gates, Jr. PBS, 2013. www.pbs.org/wnet/african-americans-many-rivers-to-cross/video/black-is-beautiful/

"Exploring the Art of Ernie Barnes." Our World with Black Enterprise, 2008. www.erniebarnes.com/black-enterprise-exploring-the-art-of-ernie-barnes.html

"Remembering Ernie Barnes." CNN, 2009. www.erniebarnes.com/cnn-remembering-ernie-barnes.html

FILM

Greenburg, Ross. *Forgotten Four: The Integration of Pro Football*. New York: Epix, 2014.

PLACES WHERE YOU CAN SEE ERNIE BARNES'S PAINTINGS

African American Museum in Philadelphia. Philadelphia, PA. www.aampmuseum.org

California African American Museum. Los Angeles, CA. www.caamuseum.org

Hilbert Museum of California Art. Orange, CA. www.hilbertmuseum.com.

Pro Football Hall of Fame. Canton, OH. www.profootballhof.com

The American Sport Art Museum & Archives. Daphne, AL. www.asama.org

QUOTE SOURCES

JACKET FLAP: "An artist paints his own reality."—Ernie Barnes, www.erniebarnes.com

PAGE 9: "Hey, man. What did Mays do today?"—Barnes, *From Pads to Palette*, p. 10.

PAGE 15: "Where are the paintings by Negro artists?"—Ernie Barnes, *The Beauty of the Ghetto: An Exhibition of Neo-Mannerist Paintings*, exhibition catalog, p. 12. New York: Grand Central Art Galleries, 1990.

PAGE 15: "Your people don't express themselves in that way"—Susan Broili, "The 'Good Times' Artist Barnes' Museum Exhibit Personal Accomplishment," *Durham Sun,* May 17, 1979.

PAGE 17: "Art is all around you. Use what you see. You catch my drift?"—Barnes, *From Pads to Palette*, p. 15.

PAGE 19: "Who is going to feed you if you become a painter?"—Steve Springer, "Barnes' World-Renowned Work Is Stroke of Genius," *Los Angeles Times*, December 16, 2001.

PAGE 20: "We are going to draft you," and "I'm going to be in the pros!"—Barnes, *From Pads to Palette*, p. 17.

PAGE 25: "You have everything but experience"—Barnes, *From Pads to Palette*, p. 28.

PAGE 27: "Negroes, Wake Up!"—Paul R. Williams, "I Am A Negro," *The American Magazine*, July 1937. (Reprinted as "Blacks Who Overcame the Odds," *Ebony*, November 1986.)

PAGE 31: "Hey, Barnes! You could be great if only you would get that art out of your head!"—Barnes, *From Pads to Palette*, p. 40.

PAGE 33 and PAGE 35: "I have a lot of work to do . . ." and "I want to become the Official Artist for the American Football League" and "When can you come to New York and bring your paintings with you?"—Barnes, *From Pads to Palette*, pp. 82, 84, 86.

PAGE 36: "It was perfect."—Attributed to Ernie Barnes, *From Pads to Palette*, p. 92.

PAGE 40: "When I became an athlete I didn't stop being an artist"—Thomas Rosandich, "A Crowning Achievement," *Official Artist of the XXIII Olympiad*, exhibition catalog, p. 4. West Hollywood, CA: The Company of Art, 1988.

"beauty and grace"—Broili, "The 'Good Times' Artist."

"America's best painter of sports"—Thomas P. Rosandich, "Ernie Barnes—'America's El Greco'— 1984 & 2004 Sport Artist of the Year." The American Sport Art Museum and Archives. www.asama.org.

PAGE 42: "Being an artist has created in me the desire to continually affirm beauty."—Barnes, *The Beauty of the Ghetto: An Exhibition of Neo-Mannerist Paintings*, exhibition catalog, p. 13. New York: Grand Central Art Galleries, 1990.

ADDITIONAL RESOURCES

Allen, Jennifer. "Colour Theory." *Frieze*, Issue 120, January 1, 2009.
www.frieze.com/article/colour-theory

Ernie Barnes: A Twentieth Century Genre Painter. Los Angeles: The Company of Art, 1971.

Haley, Alex. "Essay By Alex Haley." Ernie Barnes/Artist. *The Legacy of Alex Haley Now and Forever*, 1979. http://www.alex-haley.com/ernie_barnes_artist.htm

Touré. "A Black Picasso." *The Daily Beast,* May 1, 2009. www.thedailybeast.com/articles/2009/05/01/a-black-picasso.html

Weber, Bruce. "Ernie Barnes, Artist and Athlete, Dies at 70." *The New York Times*, April 30, 2009.

Woo, Elaine. "Ernie Barnes Dies at 70; Pro Football Player, Successful Painter." *Los Angeles Times,* April 30, 2009.

My Miss America by Ernie Barnes, 1970 • Acrylic on canvas 48 x 36 inches.
Collection of the California African American Museum
All rights reserved. Reprinted by permission.

ACKNOWLEDGMENTS

I'm grateful to the following for their expertise as I researched Ernie Barnes's life: Luz Rodriguez, Ernie Barnes Family Trust; Lynn Richardson, curator, Durham County Library, North Carolina Collections, and coordinator of Durham's Civil Rights Heritage Project; Donna Nixon of the Kathrine R. Everett Law Library, University of North Carolina; Susan Guadamuz, registrar of collections, California African American Museum; Michael Klauke, associate registrar for collections, North Carolina Museum of Art; and David Baker, president and executive director, Pro Football Hall of Fame.

—*S. N. W.*

With gratitude to Ernie Barnes for his lasting work and for opening the door to so many artists to follow in his path.

—*B. C.*